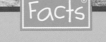

First Cookbooks

A Dinosaur
COOKBOOK

Simple Recipes for Kids

by Sarah L. Schuette

CAPSTONE PRESS
a capstone imprint

First Facts is published by Capstone Press,
1710 Roe Crest Drive, North Mankato, Minnesota 56003.
www.capstonepub.com

Books published by Capstone Press are manufactured with paper
containing at least 10 percent post-consumer waste.

Library of Congress Cataloging-in-Publication Data
Schuette, Sarah L., 1976–
  A dinosaur cookbook : simple recipes for kids / by Sarah L. Schuette.
    p. cm. — (First facts. First cookbooks)
  Includes bibliographical references and index.
  ISBN 978-1-4296-7621-2 (library binding)
  1. Cooking—Juvenile literature. 2. Dinosaurs—Juvenile literature. 3. Cookbooks. I. Title.
  TX652.5.S34355 2012
  641.5′622—dc23
                                                              2011034288

Summary: Provides instructions and step-by-step photos for making a variety of simple snacks and drinks
with a dinosaur theme.

Editorial Credits

Christine Peterson, editor; Ashlee Suker, designer; Sarah Schuette, photo stylist; Marcy Morin, studio
    scheduler; Kathy McColley, production specialist

Photo Credits

All photos by Capstone Studio/Karon Dubke except:
Shutterstock: cameilia (ferns), throughout, Tom Grundy (stone background), throughout

The author dedicates this book to her favorite dinosaur, the Tri-Sarah-Tops.

Printed in the United States of America in North Mankato, Minnesota.
062016
009823R

Table of Contents

Introduction: Triassic Hunger 4

Tools 6

Techniques 7

Fossil Tracks 8   Dino-mite Scrambler 10

Stegosaurus Salad 12   Lava Flows 14   T. Rex Teeth Pops 16

Apatosaurus Snacker 18   Jurassic Juice 20

Glossary 22

Read More 23

Internet Sites 23

Index 24

Triassic Hunger

Do you dig dinosaurs? Are you super hungry after searching for **fossils** all day? You're in luck! Consider your kitchen a new dinosaur dig site, and see what treats you can find.

Do you eat meat like megalosaurus? Perhaps you'd rather eat veggies like apatosaurus? Dig through the cupboards for the **ingredients** you'll need. Ask an adult explorer to help.

Tyrannosaurus rex had short arms that were probably never washed. But you know better. Make sure to wash your hands and clean up after yourself. The dinosaurs in your **herd** will thank you for it.

Metric Conversion Chart	
United States	**Metric**
¼ teaspoon	1.2 mL
½ teaspoon	2.5 mL
1 teaspoon	5 mL
1 tablespoon	15 mL
¼ cup	60 mL
⅓ cup	80 mL
½ cup	120 mL
⅔ cup	160 mL
¾ cup	175 mL
1 cup	240 mL
1 ounce	30 gms

Tools

Paleontologists use picks, shovels, and brushes to dig for fossils. Use this guide to prepare for your own kitchen exploration.

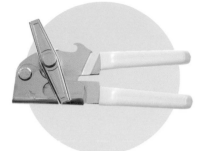

can opener—a tool used to open metal cans

cutting board—a wooden or plastic board used when slicing or chopping foods

dry-ingredient measuring cups—round cups with handles used for measuring dry ingredients

kitchen scissors—a sharp scissors used to cut food items

liquid measuring cup—a glass or plastic measuring cup with a spout for pouring

measuring spoons—spoons with small deep scoops used to measure both wet and dry ingredients

microwave-safe bowl—a non-metal bowl used to heat ingredients in a microwave

mixing bowl—a sturdy bowl used for mixing ingredients

pot holder—a thick, heavy fabric cut into a square or circle that is used to handle hot items

strainer—a bowl-shaped tool with holes in the sides and bottom used for draining liquid off food

Techniques

crack—to gently split an eggshell to release the raw egg inside

drain—to remove the liquid from something

measure—to take a specific amount of something

slice—to cut into thin pieces

spread—to cover a surface with something

sprinkle—to scatter something in small drops or bits

stir—to mix something by moving a spoon around in it

Fossil Tracks

Fossils are the only **evidence** that dinosaurs once walked the earth. You can make your own fossil tracks. They'll only last seconds instead of millions of years.

Serves 2

Ingredients:
- peanut butter
- 6 flat, round crackers
- chow mein noodles

Tools:
- spoon
- plate

1 Spread peanut butter on each cracker using a spoon.

2 Using the chow mein noodles, make dinosaur footprints on each cracker.

3 Arrange your fossil tracks on a plate and enjoy!

TIP:
You can use spreadable cheese and cashews instead to make different tracks.

Dino-mite Scrambler

It is hard work digging for dinosaur bones all day long. That's why a paleontologist needs a good breakfast.

Serves 1

Ingredients:
- 2 large eggs
- 2 tablespoons milk
- 1 teaspoon bacon bits
- 2 tablespoons shredded jack cheese

Tools:
- nonstick cooking spray, butter flavor
- microwave-safe coffee cup
- measuring spoons
- fork
- spoon

TIP:
Try adding ham and chopped onion instead of the bacon bits.

1 Spray coffee cup with cooking spray.

2 Crack eggs into cup.

3 Measure milk and add to eggs. Mix ingredients together with a fork.

4 Measure and add bacon bits and stir. Microwave cup for 45 seconds.

5 Stir egg mixture with the spoon. Measure and add cheese.

6 Microwave for 30 more seconds until eggs are puffy and not runny.

Stegosaurus Salad

Ouch! You wouldn't want to ride on a stegosaurus' back. Bony spikes and **plates** worked like armor to protect this dinosaur from **predators**. These tasty plates will protect you from hunger!

Serves 1

Ingredients:
- 1 small can pineapple rings
- 1 cup cottage cheese

Tools:
- can opener
- strainer
- two small bowls
- butter knife
- cutting board
- dry-ingredient measuring cups
- spoon
- plate

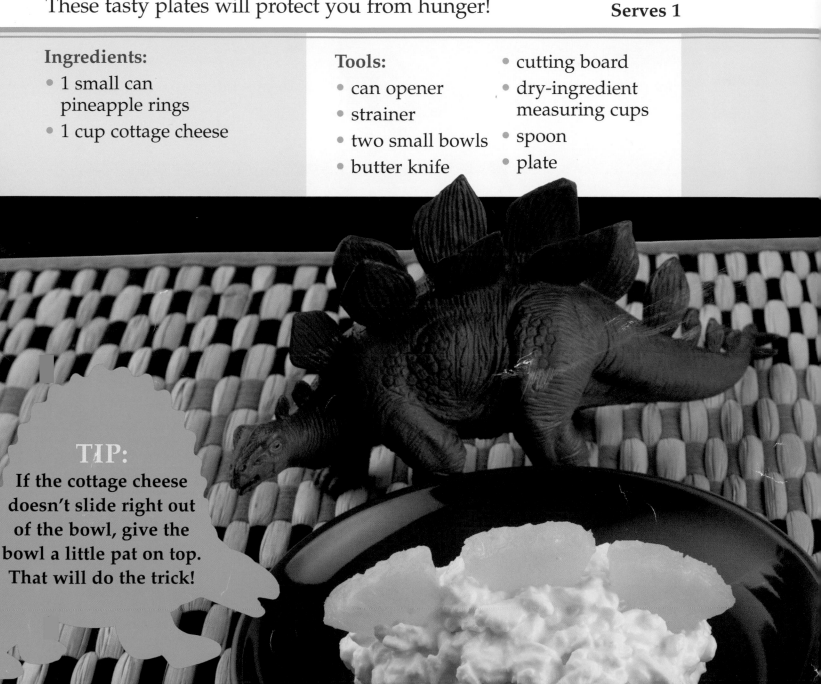

TIP:
If the cottage cheese doesn't slide right out of the bowl, give the bowl a little pat on top. That will do the trick!

1 Open can of pineapple with can opener. Using a strainer, drain the juice into a small bowl.

2 With an adult's help, slice pineapple into triangle shapes on a cutting board

3 Measure cottage cheese and place into small bowl. Press into bowl with a spoon.

4 Put the plate upside down on the bowl. Hold the bowl and plate and flip over. The cottage cheese will slide onto the plate.

5 Decorate your dinosaur body by putting the pineapple shapes down the back. The pineapple will look like steggy's plates or spikes.

TIP:
Save the drained pineapple juice and refrigerate for a cool drink.

13

Lava Flows

Red-hot lava made travel tricky for some dinosaurs. This liquid rock flowed down the sides of large volcanoes. These mini-volcanoes **erupt** with sticky sweetness.

Serves 1

Ingredients:
- 1 mini-graham cracker crust
- 1 large marshmallow
- 1 teaspoon peanut butter
- chocolate sauce
- red sprinkles

Tools:
- kitchen scissors
- knife
- microwave-safe plate

1 Remove crust from foil container. Set on microwave-safe plate.

2 Cut a hole in the middle of the marshmallow with a kitchen scissors.

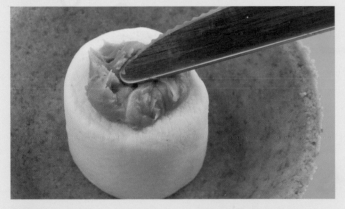

3 Using a knife, fill the hole with peanut butter.

4 Pour chocolate sauce around base of the marshmallow.

5 Sprinkle the marshmallow with red sugar. Microwave for 8-10 seconds, and watch what happens!

T. Rex Teeth Pops

T. rex munched on other dinosaurs for lunch with its huge teeth. If you put two bananas end to end, that's how long one T. rex tooth was. Wow!

Serves 2

Ingredients:
- 1 banana
- ½ cup chocolate chips

Tools:
- knife
- cutting board
- plate
- 2 craft sticks
- dry-ingredient measuring cups
- microwave-safe bowl
- spoon
- pot holders

TIP:
Sprinkle chopped nuts on top of the chocolate before it dries.

1 Peel banana. With an adult's help, cut banana in half lengthwise on a cutting board.

2 Lay both pieces, cut sides down on a plate.

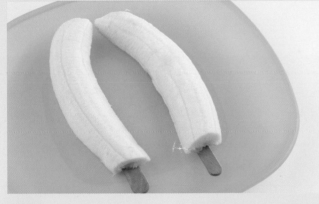

3 Insert a craft stick into cut end of each banana half. The curved part of the banana should be at the opposite end.

4 Measure chocolate chips and place into microwave-safe bowl.

5 Microwave for 40 seconds and stir until all of the chips are melted. Remove bowl using pot holders.

6 Using a spoon, spread the chocolate on the banana halves. Let sit for 30 minutes.

Apatosaurus Snacker

Apatosaurus had a super long neck to reach leaves on the tallest trees. But this dinosaur had to swallow rocks to help grind up the leaves in its stomach. Yuck! These trees will be much tastier!

Serves 4

Ingredients:
- 1 cheddar cheese stick
- prewashed spinach leaves
- 4 grapes
- 1 cup of broccoli slaw
- 4-6 dried cranberries
- 2 tablespoons sunflower seeds
- deli meat, any kind

Tools:
- plate
- dry-ingredient measuring cups
- measuring spoons
- dinosaur cookie cutter

TIP:
Drizzle your favorite dressing over your tasty salad and enjoy!

1 Lay cheese stick in the center of a plate.

2 Add spinach to the top of the cheese stick to look like leaves.

3 Place grapes on the spinach to look like fruit growing on the tree.

4 Measure broccoli slaw, and sprinkle over the bottom of the plate to look like grass.

5 Next add the cranberries and sunflower seeds on the slaw to look like different rocks.

6 Use a cookie cutter to cut dinosaur shapes out of deli meat and add to your leafy scene.

Jurassic Juice

Fossil hunters find dinosaur bones in many different places, even in ice! Now you can uncover your own frosty dinos with this cool drink.

Serves 1

Ingredients:
- 4 gummy dinosaurs
- ½ cup apple juice
- ½ cup grape juice
- ¼ cup frozen lemonade concentrate
- ¼ cup ginger ale

Tools:
- ice cube tray
- liquid measuring cup
- tall glass
- spoon

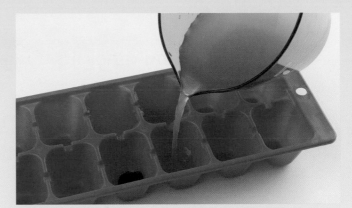

 1 In an ice cube tray, place one gummy dinosaur into each of four cubes.

 2 Fill each of the four cubes with apple juice. Freeze for two to three hours.

3 Measure and pour grape juice, lemonade, and ginger ale into a tall glass. Stir with a spoon.

4 Add the dinosaur ice cubes to the glass.

Glossary

erupt (i-RUHPT)—to suddenly burst; a volcano shoots steam, lava, and ash into the air when it erupts

evidence (EV-uh-duhnss)—information, items, and facts that help prove something to be true or false

fossil (FAH-suhl)—the remains or traces of an animal or a plant preserved as rock

herd (HURD)—a large group of animals that lives or moves together

ingredient (in-GREE-dee-uhnt)—an item used to make something else

paleontologist (pale-ee-uhn-TOL-uh-gist)—a person who studies the science of fossils and other ancient life forms such as dinosaurs

plate (PLAYT)—a flat, bony growth

predator (PRED-uh-tur)—an animal that hunts other animals for food

Read More

Llewellyn, Claire. *Cooking with Fruits and Vegetables.* Cooking Healthy. New York: Rosen Central, 2012.

Schuette, Sarah L. *A Monster Cookbook: Simple Recipes for Kids.* First Cookbooks. Mankato, Minn.: Capstone Press, 2011.

Tuminelly, Nancy. *Cool Sandwich Food Art: Easy Recipes that Make Food Fun to Eat!* Cool Food Art. Edina, Minn.: ABDO Pub. Company, 2011.

Internet Sites

FactHound offers a safe, fun way to find Internet sites related to this book. All of the sites on FactHound have been researched by our staff.

Here's all you do:

Visit *www.facthound.com*

Type in this code: 9781429676212

Super-cool stuff! Check out projects, games and lots more at **www.capstonekids.com**

Index

Apatosaurus Snacker, 18–19

Dino-mite Scrambler, 10–11

fossils, 4, 6, 8, 20
Fossil Tracks, 8–9

herds, 4

ingredients, 4

Lava Flows, 14–15

metric guide, 4

palentologists, 6, 10

Stegosaurus Salad, 12–13

T. Rex Teeth Pops, 16–17